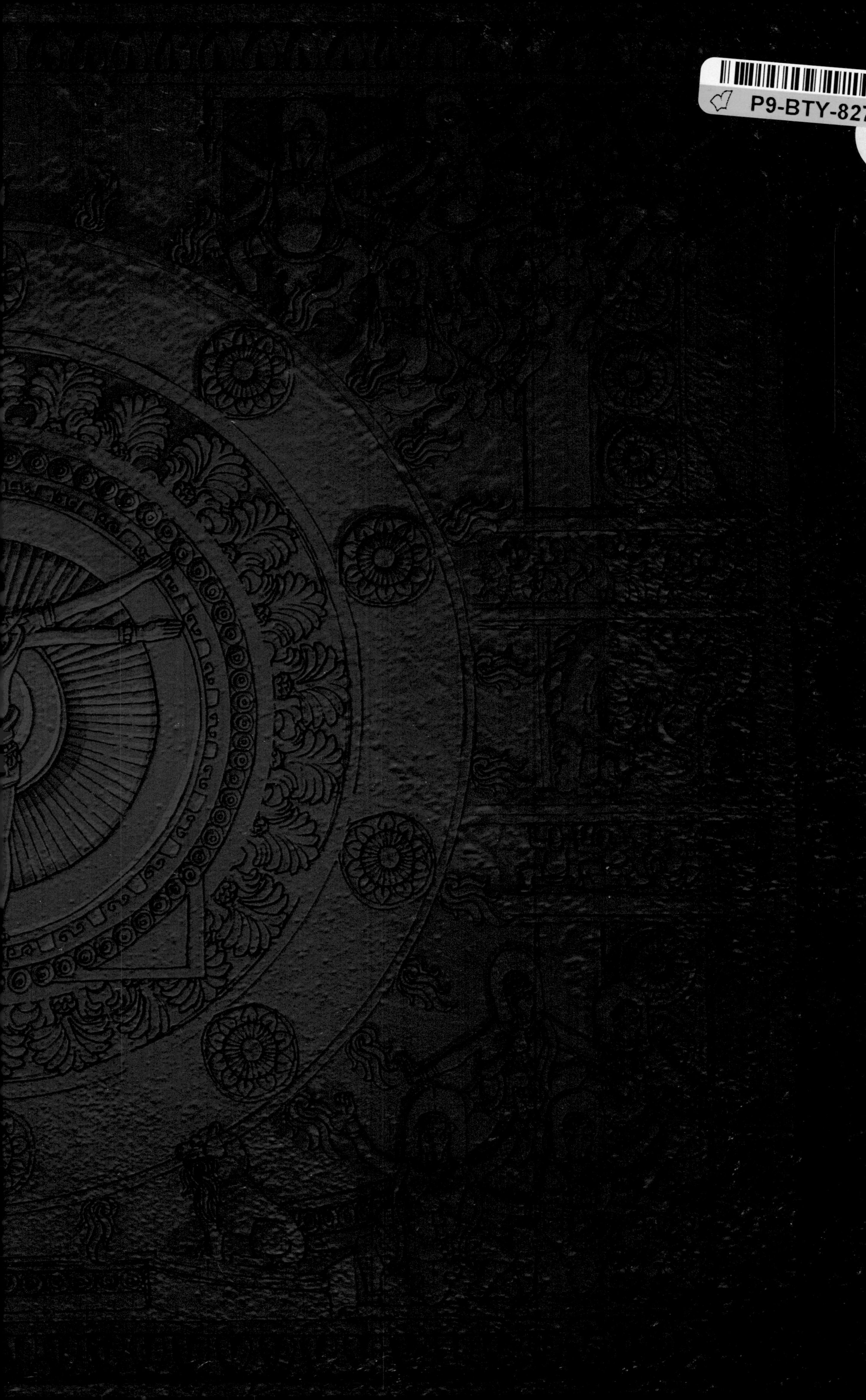

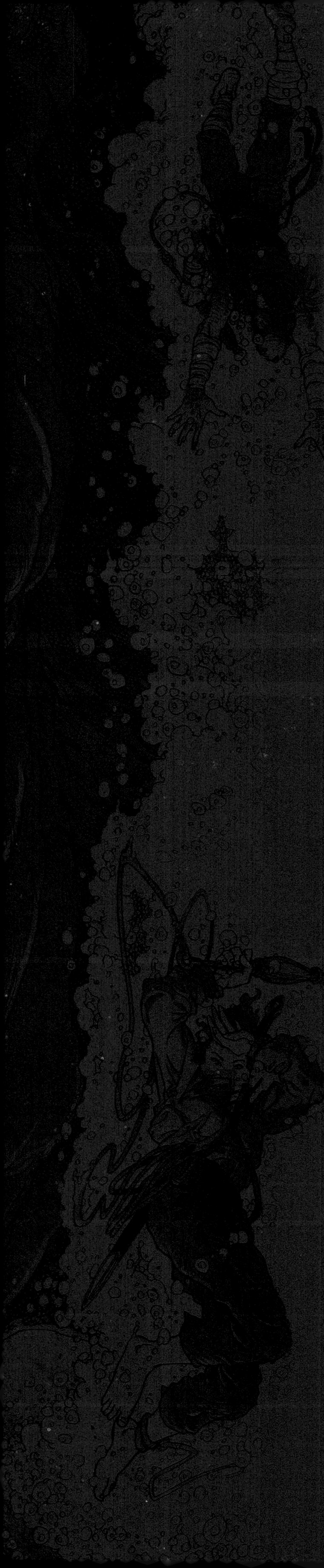

"He paused above our dwellings; he ravened around our sevenfold portals with spears athirst for blood; but he went hence, or ever his jaws were glutted with our gore, or the Fire-god's pine-fed flame had seized our crown of towers. So fierce was the noise of battle raised behind him, a thing too hard for him to conquer, as he wrestled with his dragon foe."

-- From Sophocles' Antigone.

"If you see only leaves on a plant, know that it contains within the power to bear fruit and flowers (...) thus, teach your students not to invent things, but to see them as they are."

-- From Darius' third discourse to the Council

 www.humanoids-publishing.com

Translation by Justin Kelly

Book Designer: Thierry Frissen
Letterer: Jason Wahler
Managing Editor: Paul Benjamin
Marketing Manager: Ian Sattler
Circulation: Sue Hartung
Original French Version Edited by: Philippe Hauri
Publisher: Fabrice Giger

MORGANA#1: HEAVEN'S GATE

Humanoids Publishing PO Box 931658, Hollywood, CA 90093

Printed and bound in Belgium.

ISBN: 1-930652-32-1

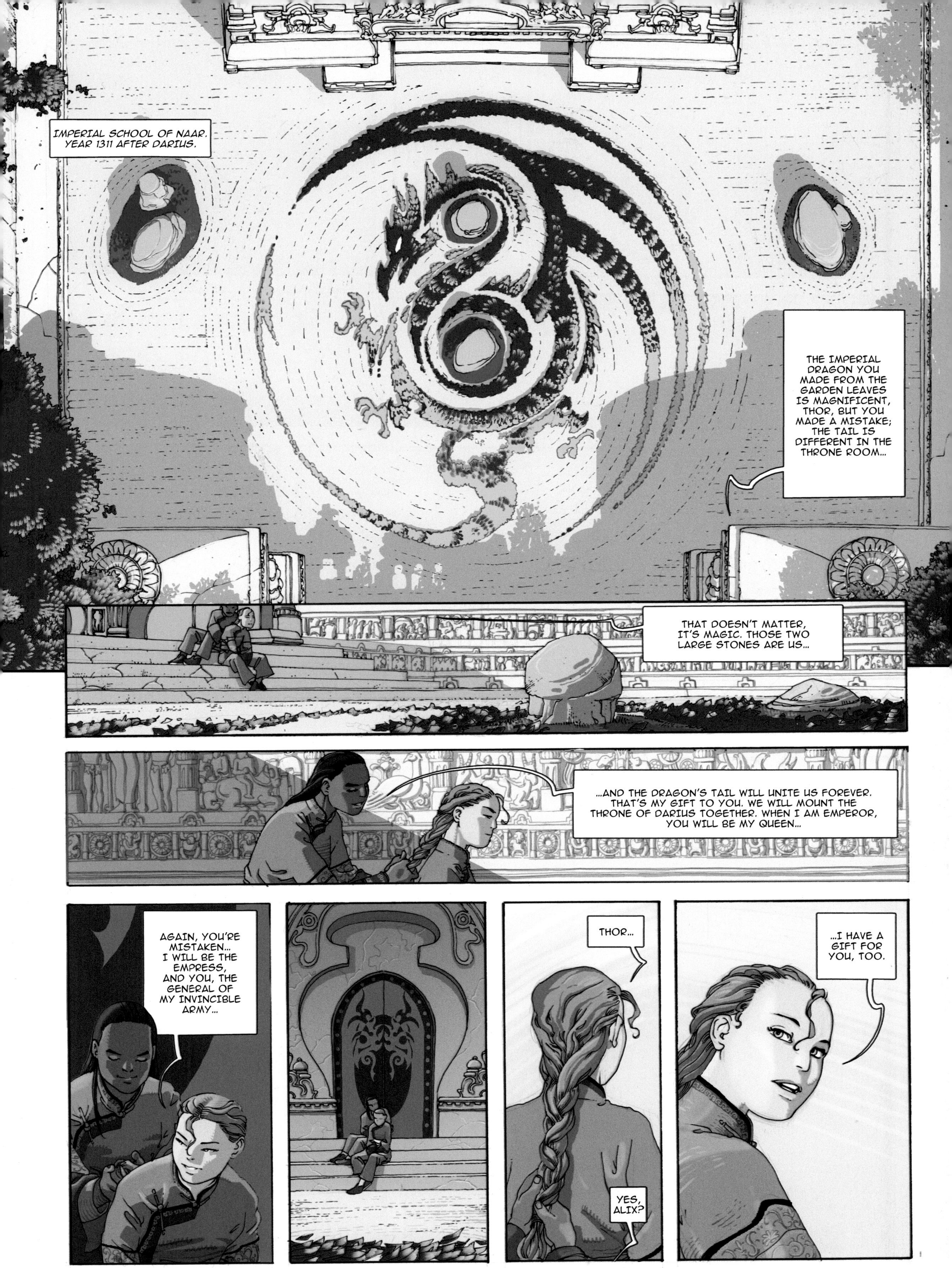
IMPERIAL SCHOOL OF NAAR. YEAR 1311 AFTER DARIUS.
THE IMPERIAL DRAGON YOU MADE FROM THE GARDEN LEAVES IS MAGNIFICENT, THOR, BUT YOU MADE A MISTAKE; THE TAIL IS DIFFERENT IN THE THRONE ROOM...
THAT DOESN'T MATTER, IT'S MAGIC. THOSE TWO LARGE STONES ARE US...
...AND THE DRAGON'S TAIL WILL UNITE US FOREVER. THAT'S MY GIFT TO YOU. WE WILL MOUNT THE THRONE OF DARIUS TOGETHER. WHEN I AM EMPEROR, YOU WILL BE MY QUEEN...
AGAIN, YOU'RE MISTAKEN... I WILL BE THE EMPRESS, AND YOU, THE GENERAL OF MY INVINCIBLE ARMY...
THOR...
YES, ALIX?
...I HAVE A GIFT FOR YOU, TOO.

I WILL KEEP IT ALWAYS.

WHOOoSSH!!
ALIX! THOR!

COME QUICKLY! IT'S LATE, AND THE OTHER STUDENTS ARE ALREADY IN THE THEATER.

HA HA! CATCH ME IF YOU CAN!

YOU TWO ARE INSEPARABLE. HURRY, RUN!

HA HA!

?

HURRY! SOPHOCLES WON'T WAIT FOR YOU, AND ANTIGONE'S TRAGEDY WILL BE OVER BEFORE YOU HAVE A CHANCE TO LEARN FROM IT!

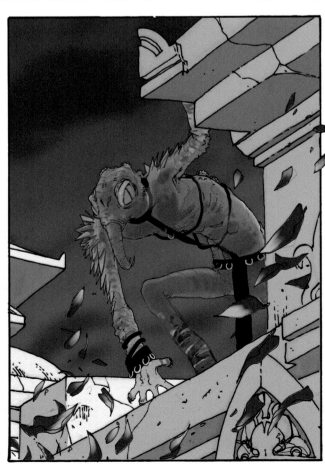

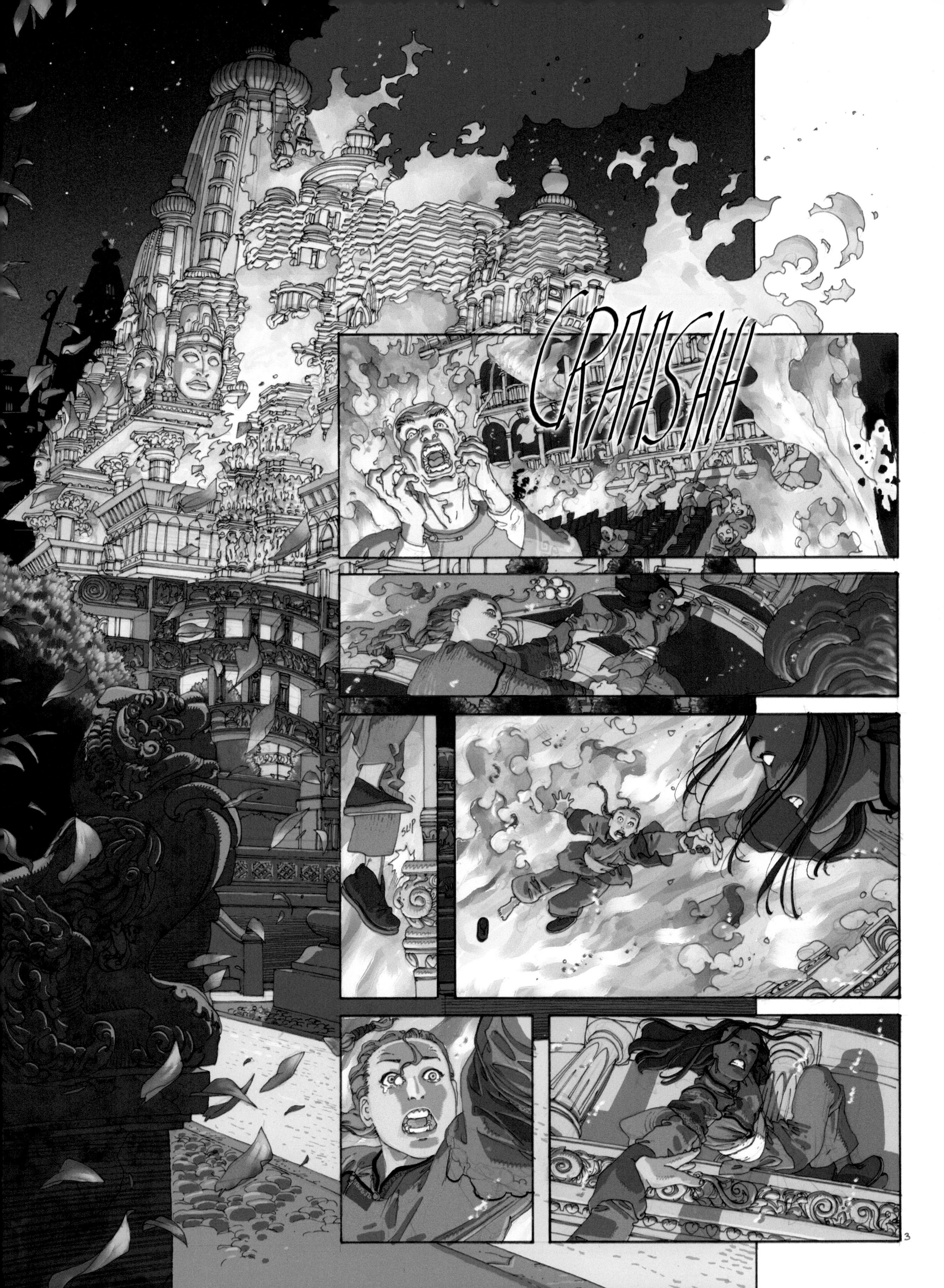
CRAASHH
SLIP

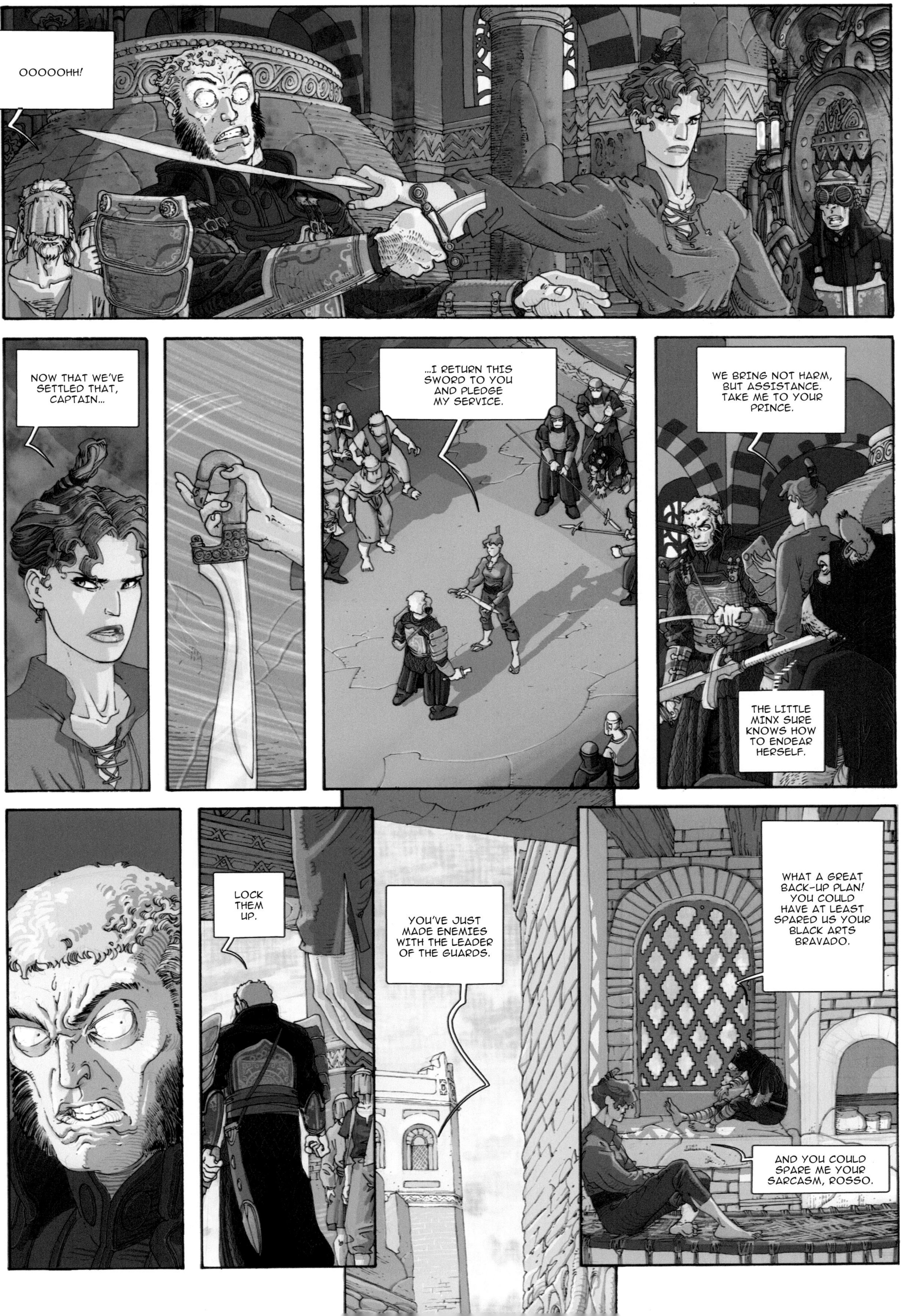
OOOOOHH!
NOW THAT WE'VE SETTLED THAT, CAPTAIN...
...I RETURN THIS SWORD TO YOU AND PLEDGE MY SERVICE.
WE BRING NOT HARM, BUT ASSISTANCE. TAKE ME TO YOUR PRINCE.
THE LITTLE MINX SURE KNOWS HOW TO ENDEAR HERSELF.
LOCK THEM UP.
YOU'VE JUST MADE ENEMIES WITH THE LEADER OF THE GUARDS.
WHAT A GREAT BACK-UP PLAN! YOU COULD HAVE AT LEAST SPARED US YOUR BLACK ARTS BRAVADO.
AND YOU COULD SPARE ME YOUR SARCASM, ROSSO.

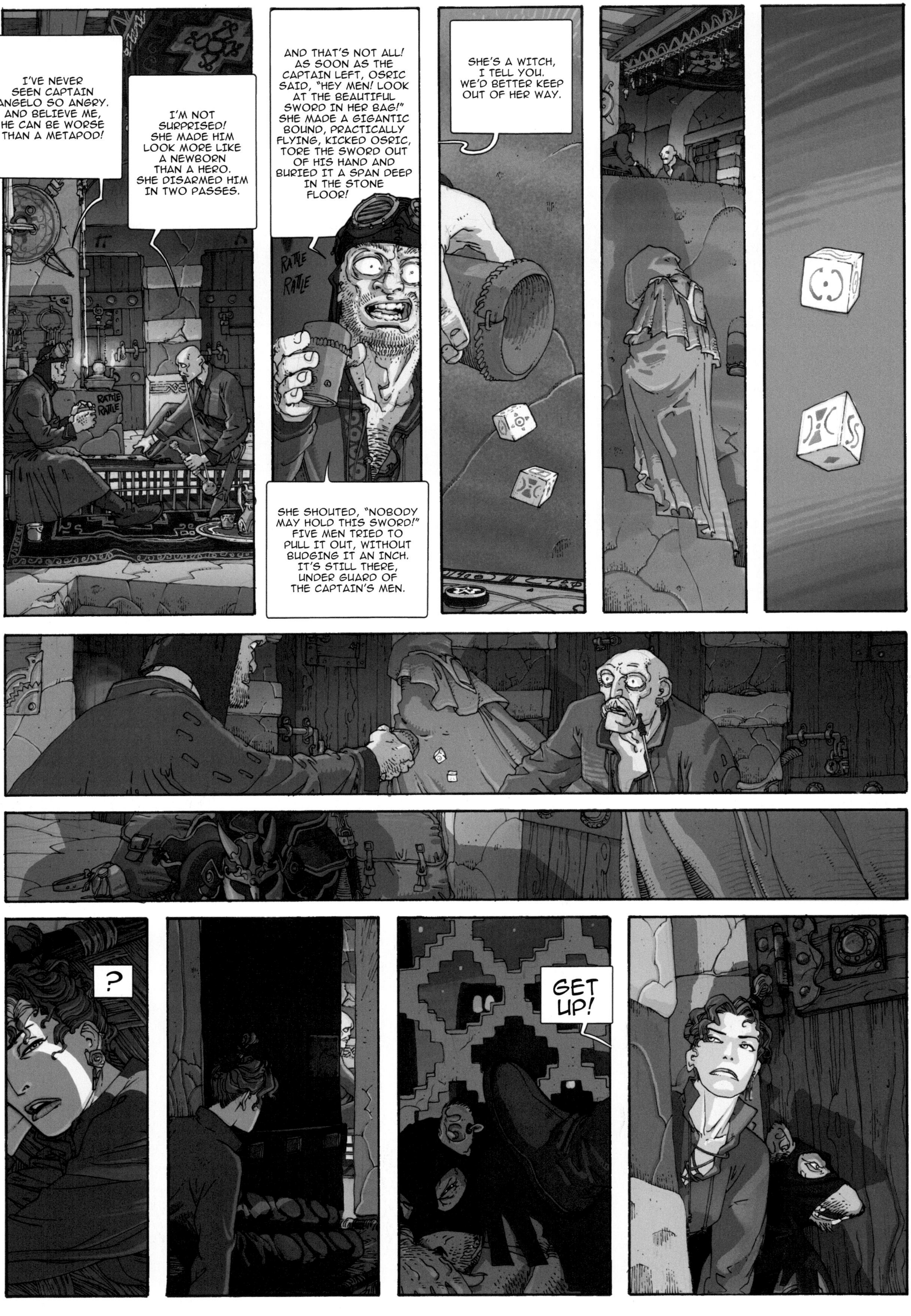

I'VE NEVER SEEN CAPTAIN ANGELO SO ANGRY. AND BELIEVE ME, HE CAN BE WORSE THAN A METAPOD!
I'M NOT SURPRISED! SHE MADE HIM LOOK MORE LIKE A NEWBORN THAN A HERO. SHE DISARMED HIM IN TWO PASSES.
RATTLE RATTLE
AND THAT'S NOT ALL! AS SOON AS THE CAPTAIN LEFT, OSRIC SAID, "HEY MEN! LOOK AT THE BEAUTIFUL SWORD IN HER BAG!" SHE MADE A GIGANTIC BOUND, PRACTICALLY FLYING, KICKED OSRIC, TORE THE SWORD OUT OF HIS HAND AND BURIED IT A SPAN DEEP IN THE STONE FLOOR!
RATTLE RATTLE
SHE SHOUTED, "NOBODY MAY HOLD THIS SWORD!" FIVE MEN TRIED TO PULL IT OUT, WITHOUT BUDGING IT AN INCH. IT'S STILL THERE, UNDER GUARD OF THE CAPTAIN'S MEN.
SHE'S A WITCH, I TELL YOU. WE'D BETTER KEEP OUT OF HER WAY.
?
GET UP!

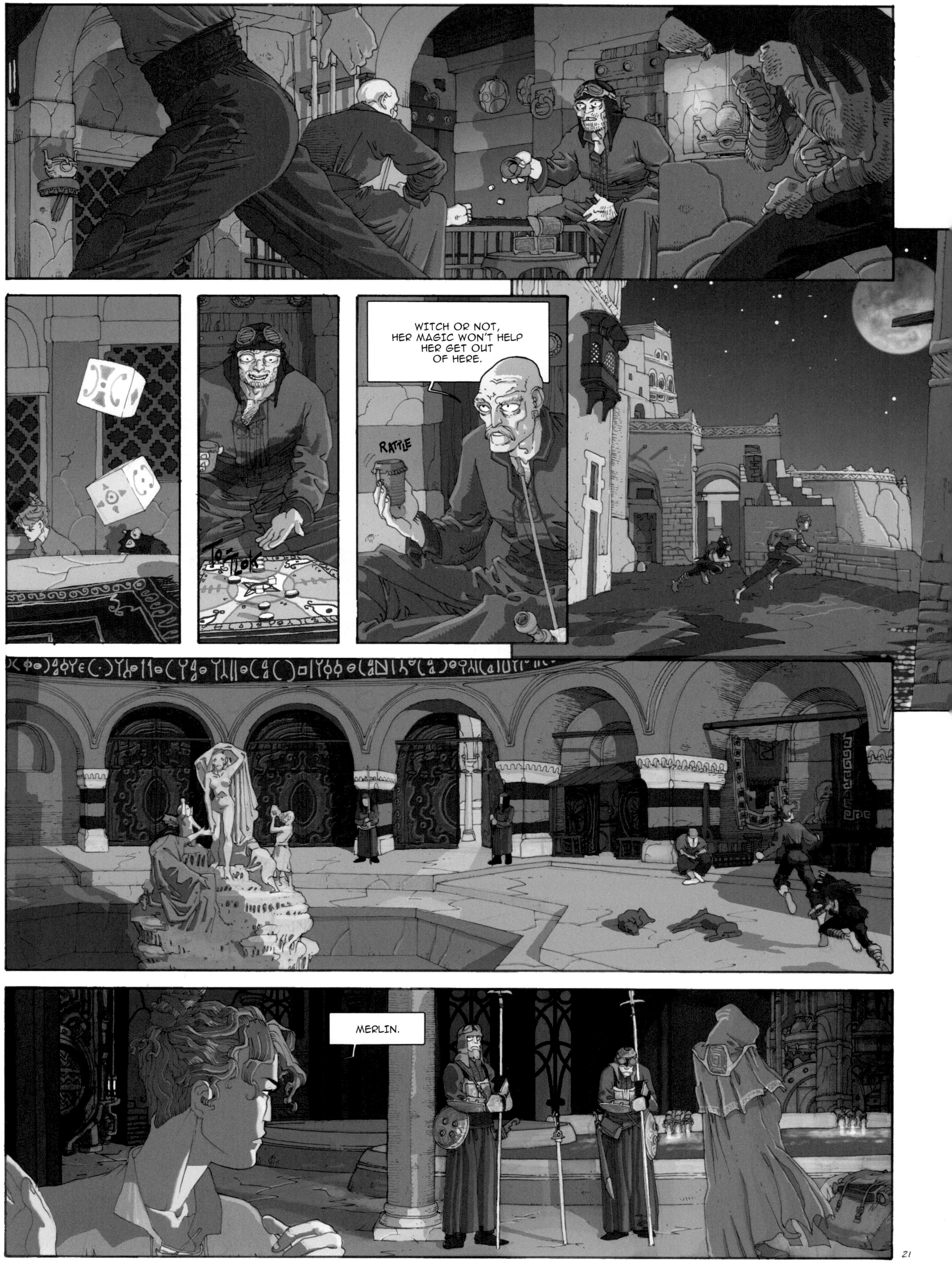

TOC-TLOK
WITCH OR NOT, HER MAGIC WON'T HELP HER GET OUT OF HERE.
RATTLE
MERLIN.

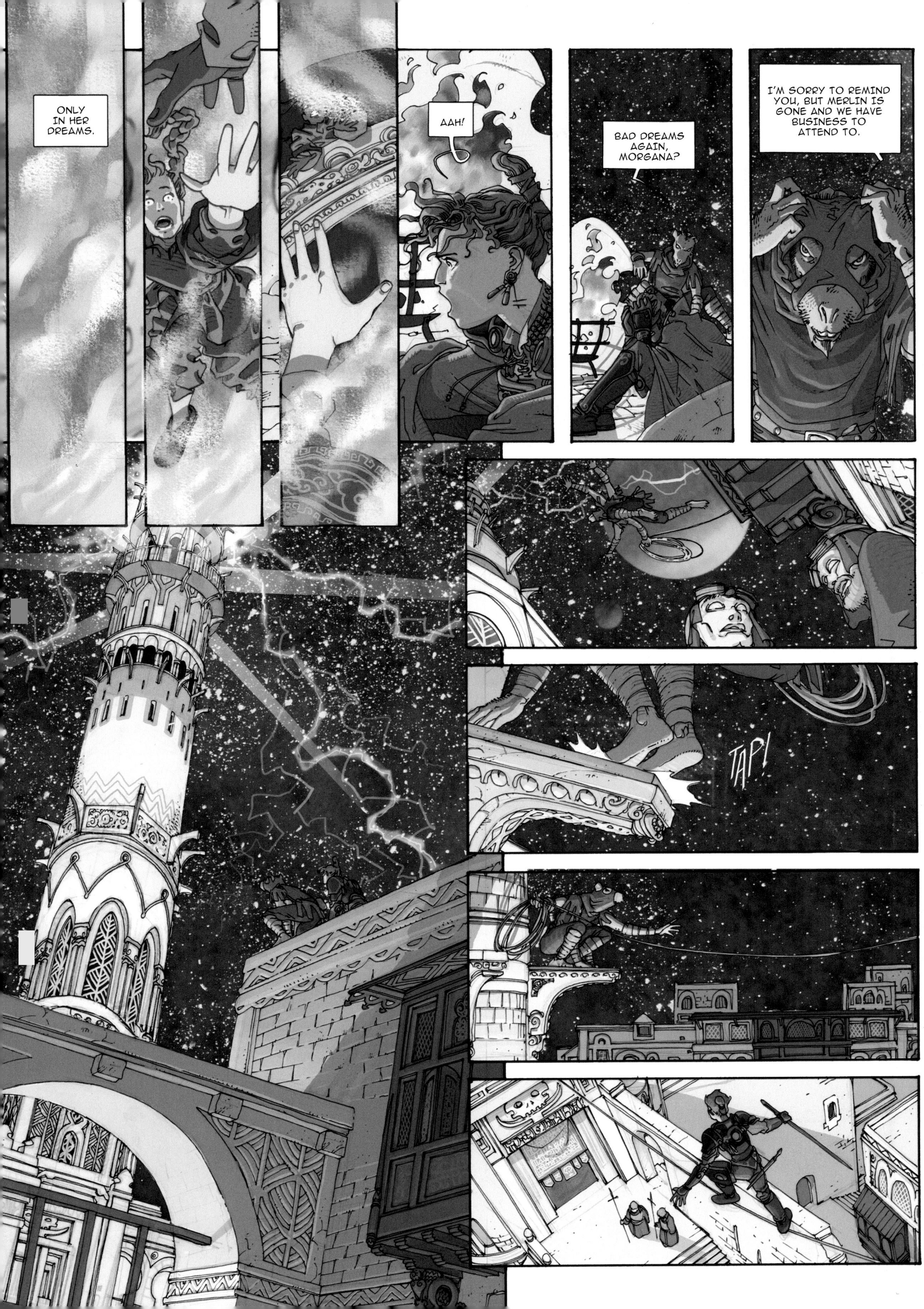
ONLY IN HER DREAMS.
AAH!
BAD DREAMS AGAIN, MORGANA?
I'M SORRY TO REMIND YOU, BUT MERLIN IS GONE AND WE HAVE BUSINESS TO ATTEND TO.
TAP!

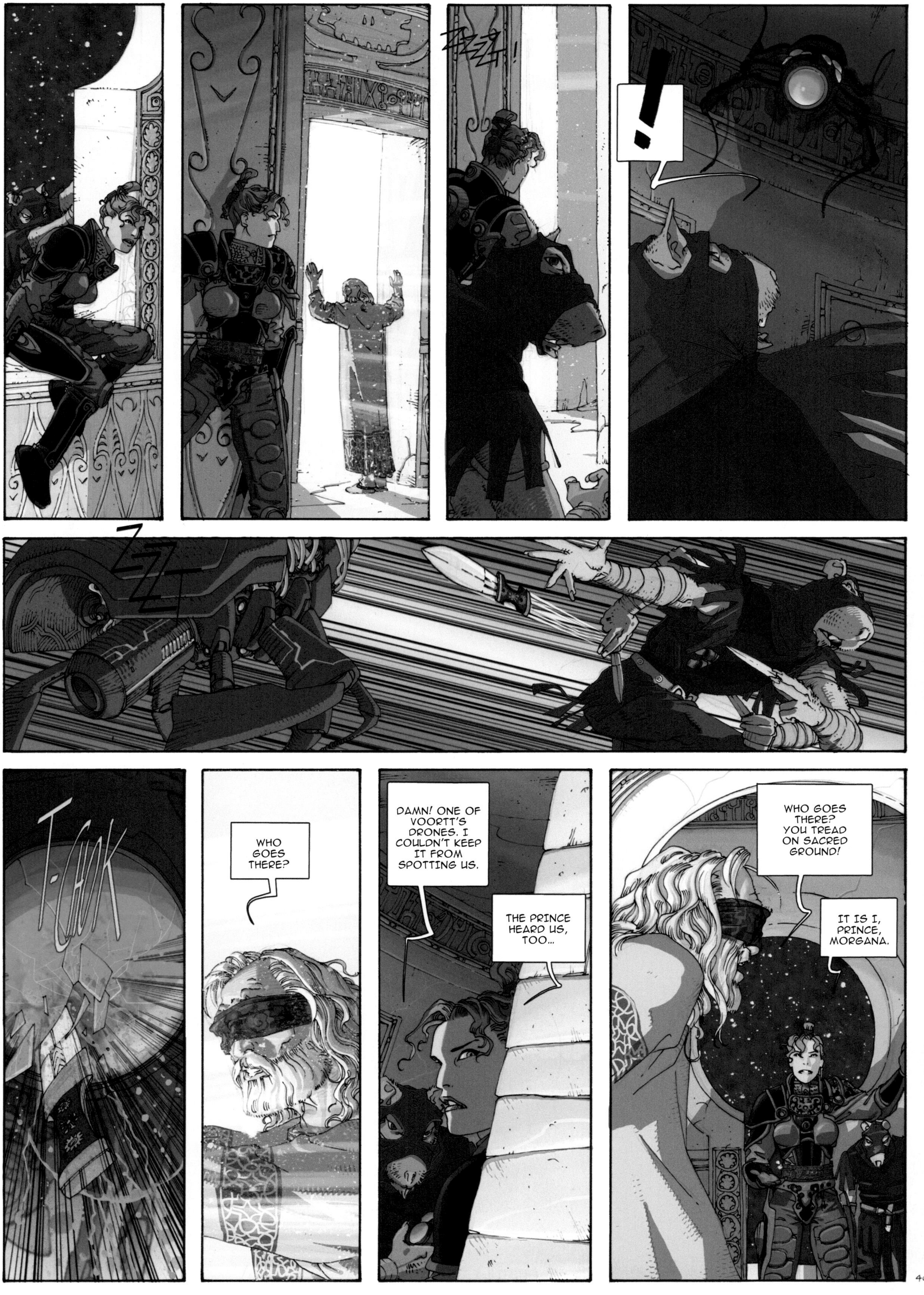
ZZZT!
!
ZZZ
T-CHOK
WHO GOES THERE?
DAMN! ONE OF VOORTT'S DRONES. I COULDN'T KEEP IT FROM SPOTTING US.
THE PRINCE HEARD US, TOO...
WHO GOES THERE? YOU TREAD ON SACRED GROUND!
IT IS I, PRINCE, MORGANA.

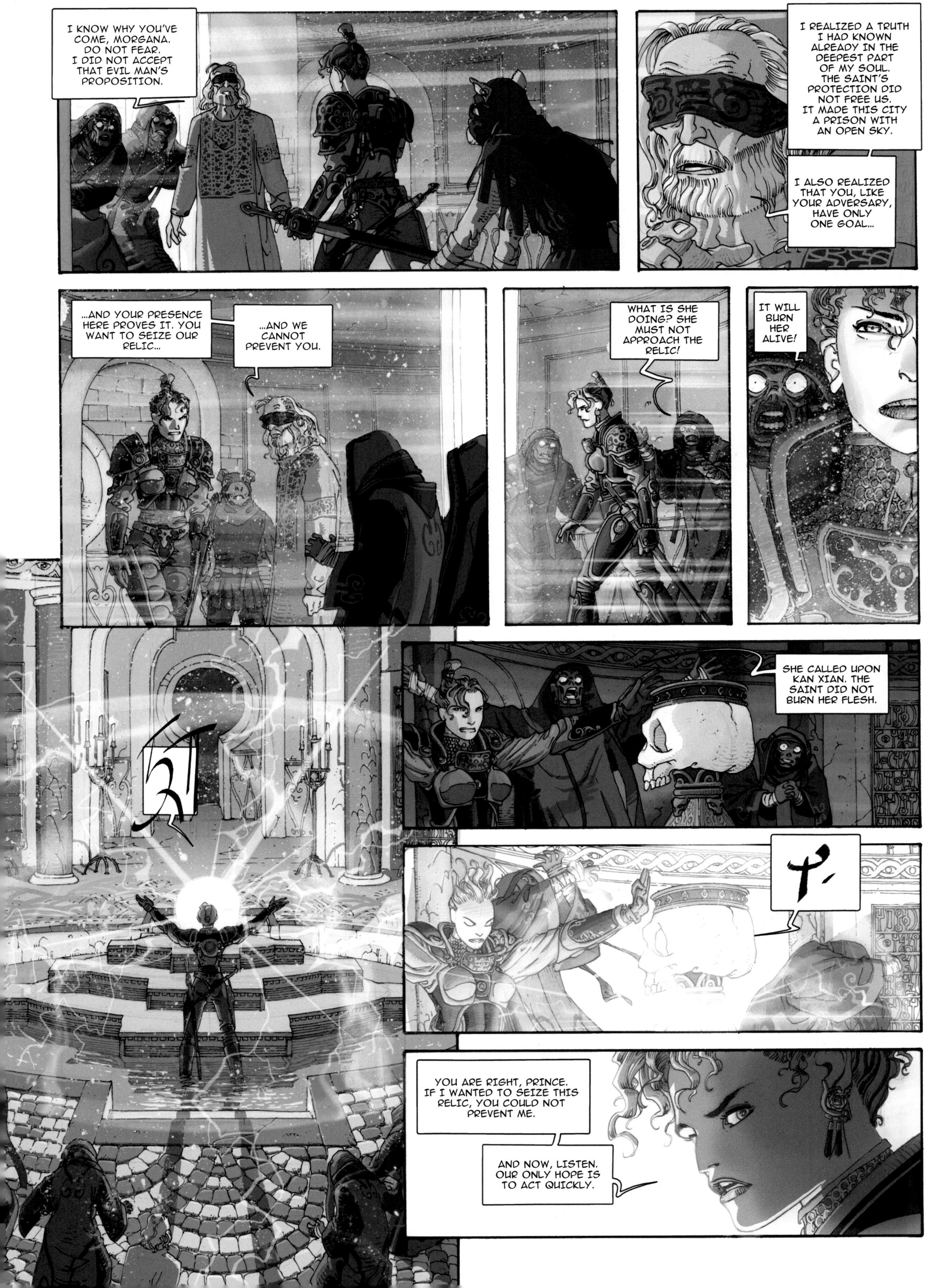
I KNOW WHY YOU'VE COME, MORGANA. DO NOT FEAR. I DID NOT ACCEPT THAT EVIL MAN'S PROPOSITION.
I REALIZED A TRUTH I HAD KNOWN ALREADY IN THE DEEPEST PART OF MY SOUL. THE SAINT'S PROTECTION DID NOT FREE US. IT MADE THIS CITY A PRISON WITH AN OPEN SKY.
I ALSO REALIZED THAT YOU, LIKE YOUR ADVERSARY, HAVE ONLY ONE GOAL...
...AND YOUR PRESENCE HERE PROVES IT. YOU WANT TO SEIZE OUR RELIC...
...AND WE CANNOT PREVENT YOU.
WHAT IS SHE DOING? SHE MUST NOT APPROACH THE RELIC!
IT WILL BURN HER ALIVE!
SHE CALLED UPON KAN XIAN. THE SAINT DID NOT BURN HER FLESH.
YOU ARE RIGHT, PRINCE. IF I WANTED TO SEIZE THIS RELIC, YOU COULD NOT PREVENT ME.
AND NOW, LISTEN. OUR ONLY HOPE IS TO ACT QUICKLY.

THOR...

YES, ALIX?

I HAVE A GIFT FOR YOU, TOO...

COMMANDER.

THE DRONE IN THE TOWER WAS JUST DESTROYED.

WHAT?

HERE'S THE LAST IMAGE WE RECEIVED BEFORE THE SIGNAL WAS LOST.

IT'S THAT KRRITT! THEY MUST HAVE GONE INTO THE TOWER TO STEAL THE ARCANE!

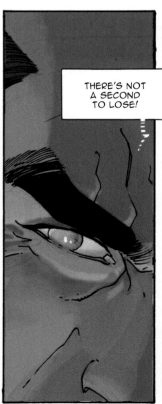

THERE'S NOT A SECOND TO LOSE!

SMOLDERING ARROWS! THEY'RE SURROUNDING THEIR WALLS WITH SMOKE!

THE ARCANE STILL PROTECTS THE CITY... PERHAPS MORGANA FAILED TO STEAL THE ARCANE. OR PERHAPS SHE HAS ANOTHER PLAN...

IT DOES NOT MATTER. I WILL ACT IN THE OPEN THIS TIME. TO HELL WITH THE IMPERIAL EMBARGO.

IMPERIAL PROBES SCAN THE FIELD. SURELY THEY'VE DETECTED MY DRONES BY NOW.

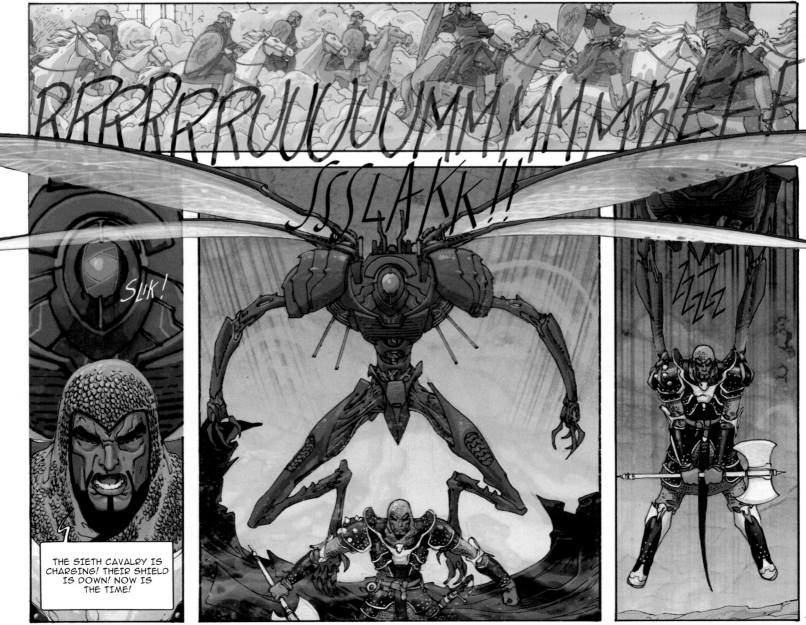

RRRRRRUUUUUMMMMMMBBLEE!

SSSLAKK!!

SLIK!

ZZZ

THE SIETH CAVALRY IS CHARGING! THEIR SHIELD IS DOWN! NOW IS THE TIME!

WHOOGSHBOOM

THE SIETH ARE HEADING FOR OUR EAST ARTILLERY, UNDER COVER OF THE SMOKE.

BOOM

WE'RE SAFE HERE...

RELOAD THE CANNON, AND PREPARE TO FIRE WHEN THE SMOKE CLEARS!

UGH!

HURRY! THE WIND IS DISPERSING OUR COVER!

POINT THE CANNONS TOWARDS THE TARGET!

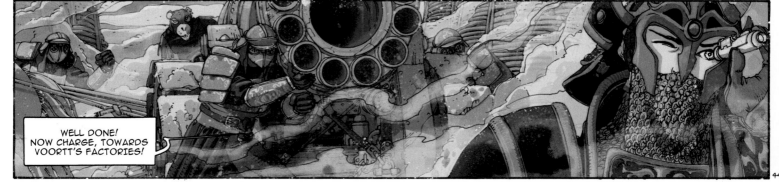

WELL DONE! NOW CHARGE, TOWARDS VOORTT'S FACTORIES!

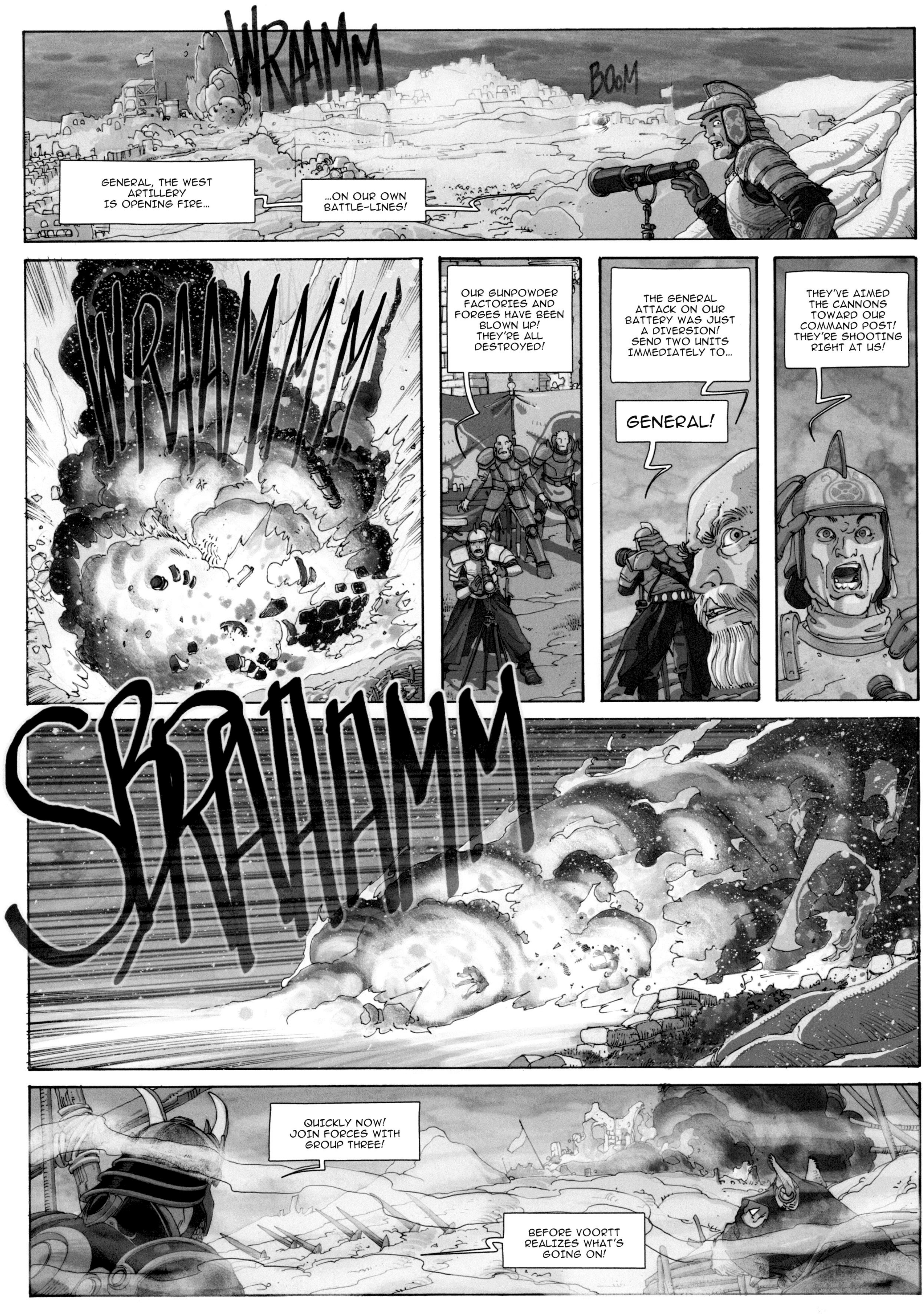

WRAAMM
BOOM
GENERAL, THE WEST ARTILLERY IS OPENING FIRE...
...ON OUR OWN BATTLE-LINES!
WRAAMMM
OUR GUNPOWDER FACTORIES AND FORGES HAVE BEEN BLOWN UP! THEY'RE ALL DESTROYED!
THE GENERAL ATTACK ON OUR BATTERY WAS JUST A DIVERSION! SEND TWO UNITS IMMEDIATELY TO...
GENERAL!
THEY'VE AIMED THE CANNONS TOWARD OUR COMMAND POST! THEY'RE SHOOTING RIGHT AT US!
SBRAAAMM
QUICKLY NOW! JOIN FORCES WITH GROUP THREE!
BEFORE VOORTT REALIZES WHAT'S GOING ON!

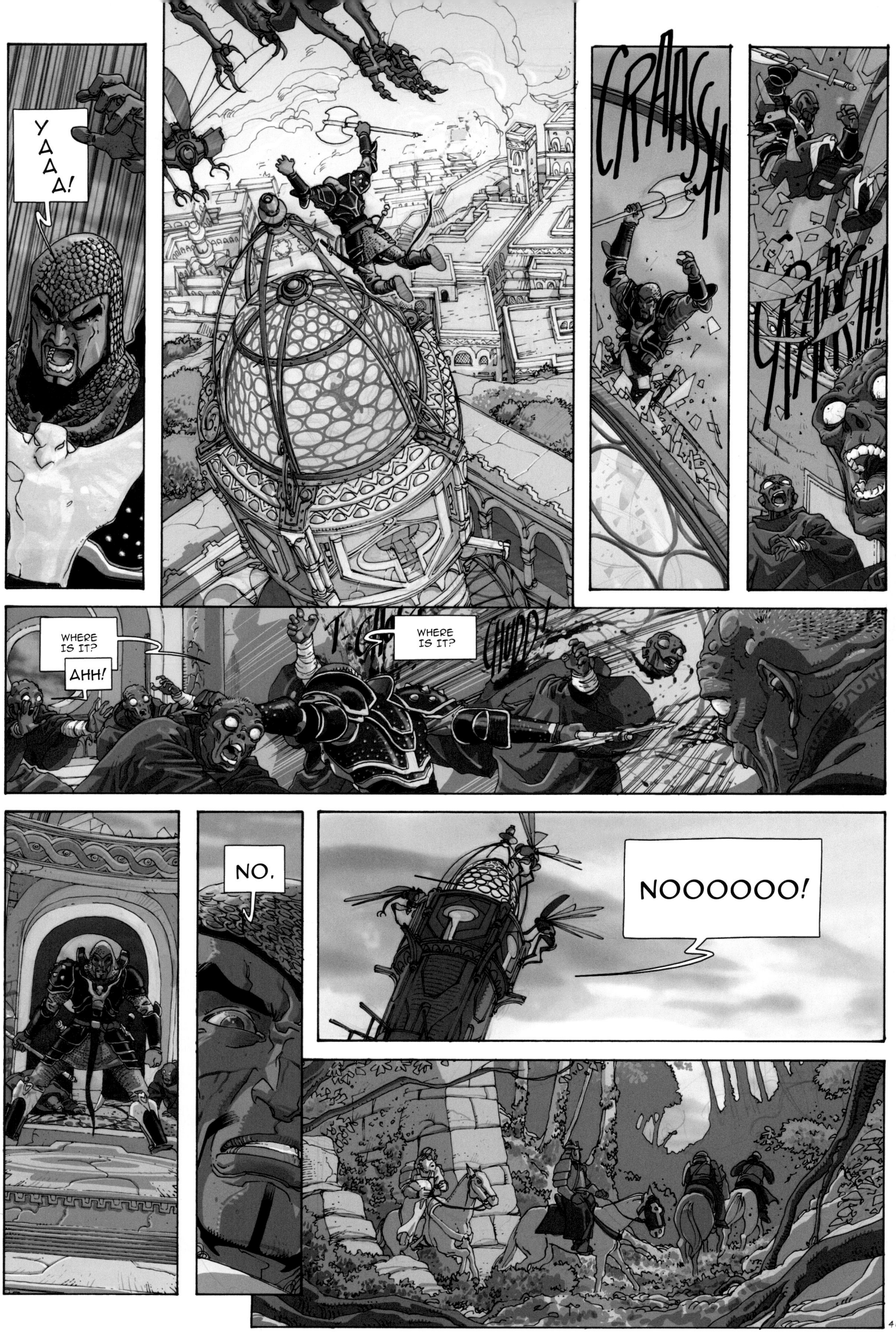

YAAA!
CRAASCH
WHERE IS IT?
AHH!
WHERE IS IT?
CHUDD!
NO.
NOOOOOO!

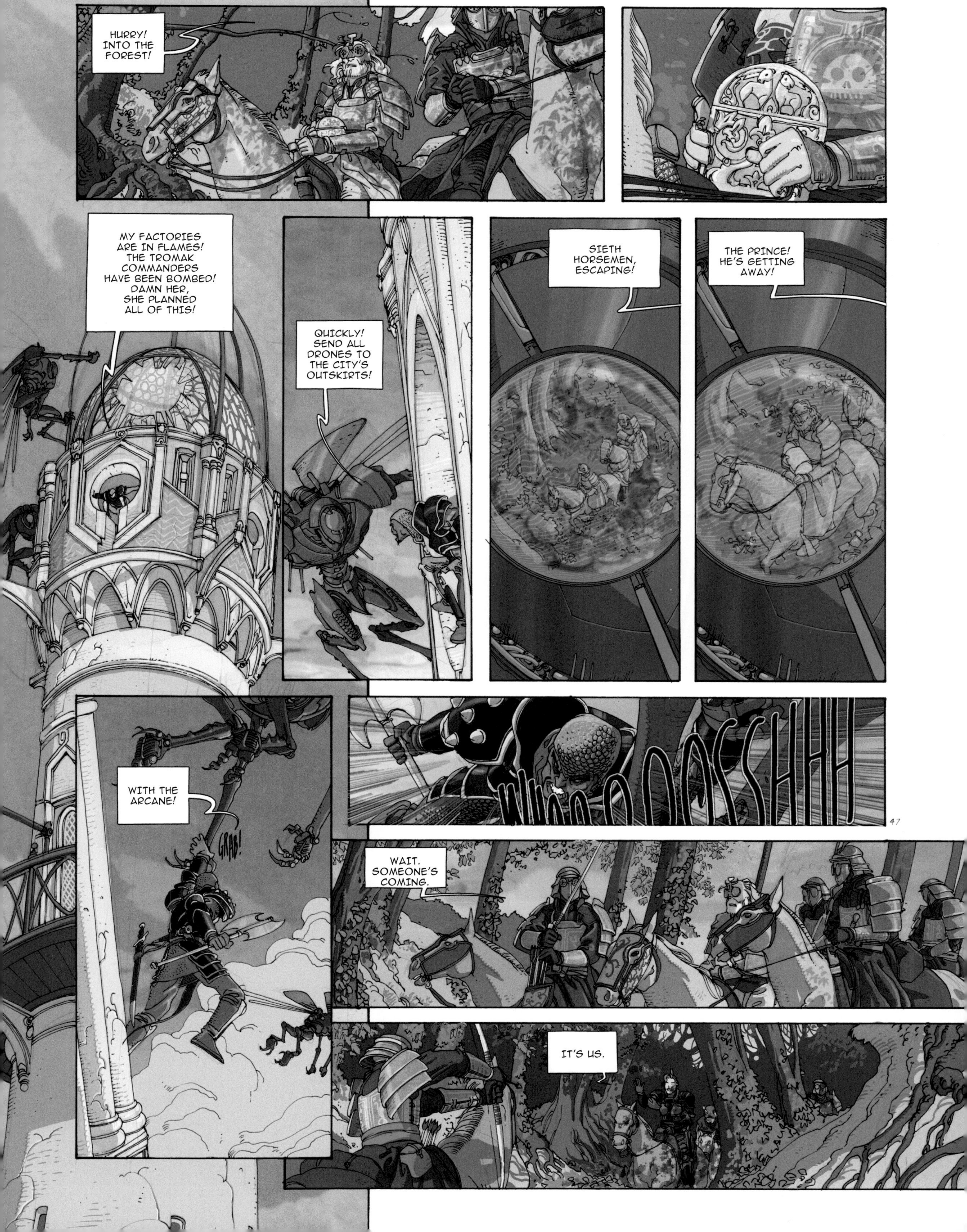
HURRY! INTO THE FOREST!
MY FACTORIES ARE IN FLAMES! THE TROMAK COMMANDERS HAVE BEEN BOMBED! DAMN HER, SHE PLANNED ALL OF THIS!
QUICKLY! SEND ALL DRONES TO THE CITY'S OUTSKIRTS!
SIETH HORSEMEN, ESCAPING!
THE PRINCE! HE'S GETTING AWAY!
WITH THE ARCANE!
GRAB!
WHOOOOOSSHHH
WAIT. SOMEONE'S COMING.
IT'S US.

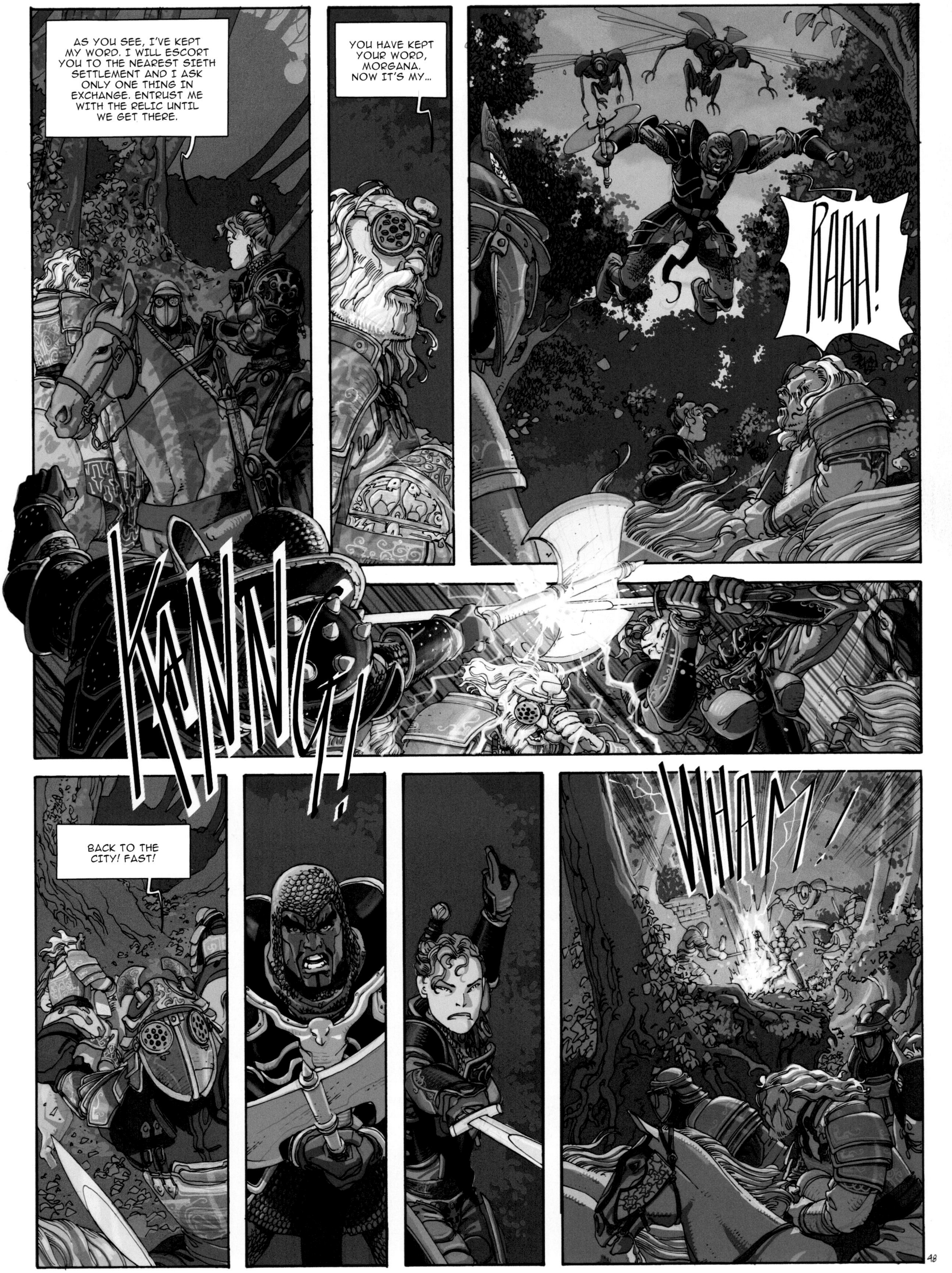
AS YOU SEE, I'VE KEPT MY WORD. I WILL ESCORT YOU TO THE NEAREST SIETH SETTLEMENT AND I ASK ONLY ONE THING IN EXCHANGE. ENTRUST ME WITH THE RELIC UNTIL WE GET THERE.
YOU HAVE KEPT YOUR WORD, MORGANA. NOW IT'S MY...
RAAA!
KANNG!
BACK TO THE CITY! FAST!
WHAM!

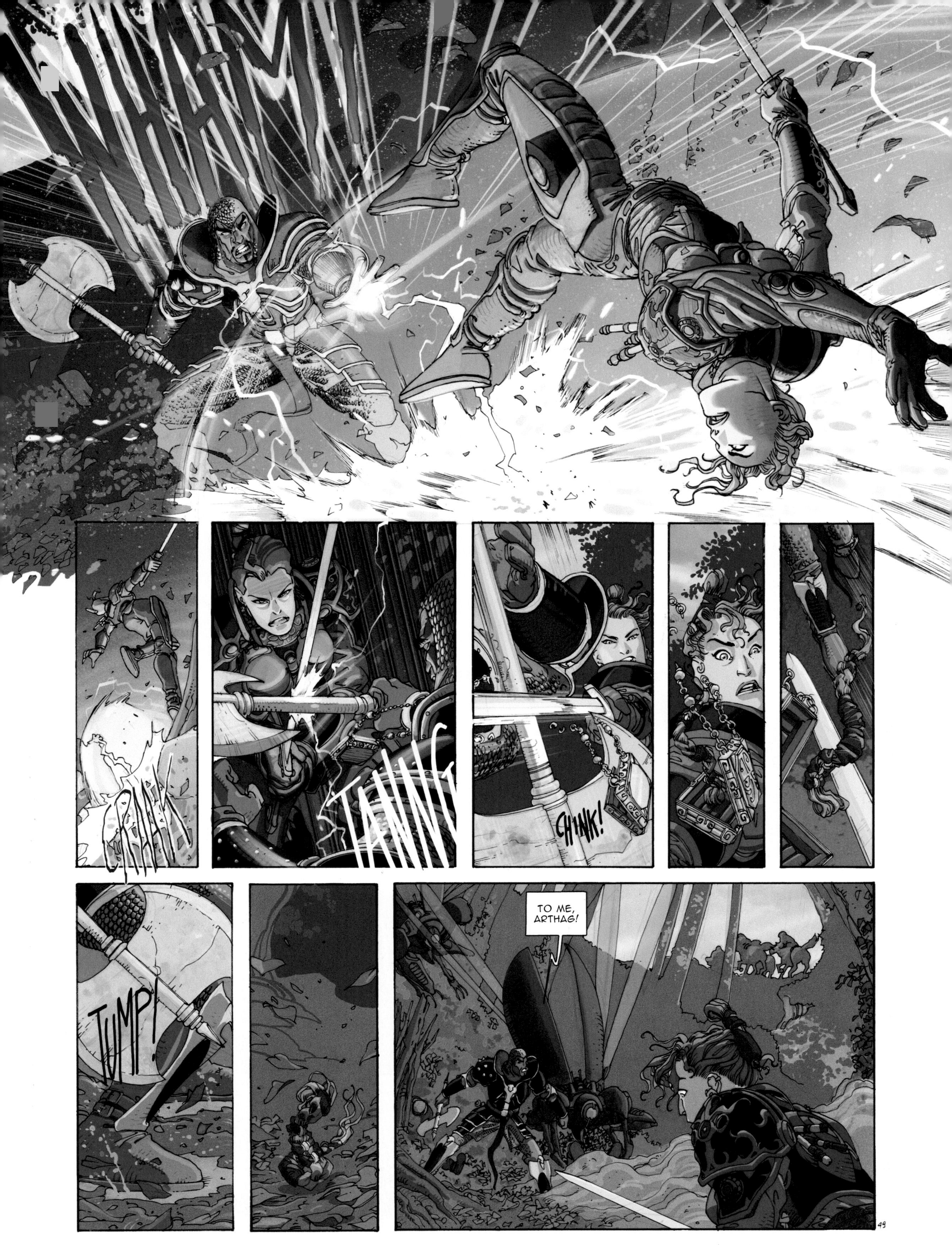
WHAM!
CRAAK
TANNG
CHINK!
TUMP!
TO ME, ARTHAG!

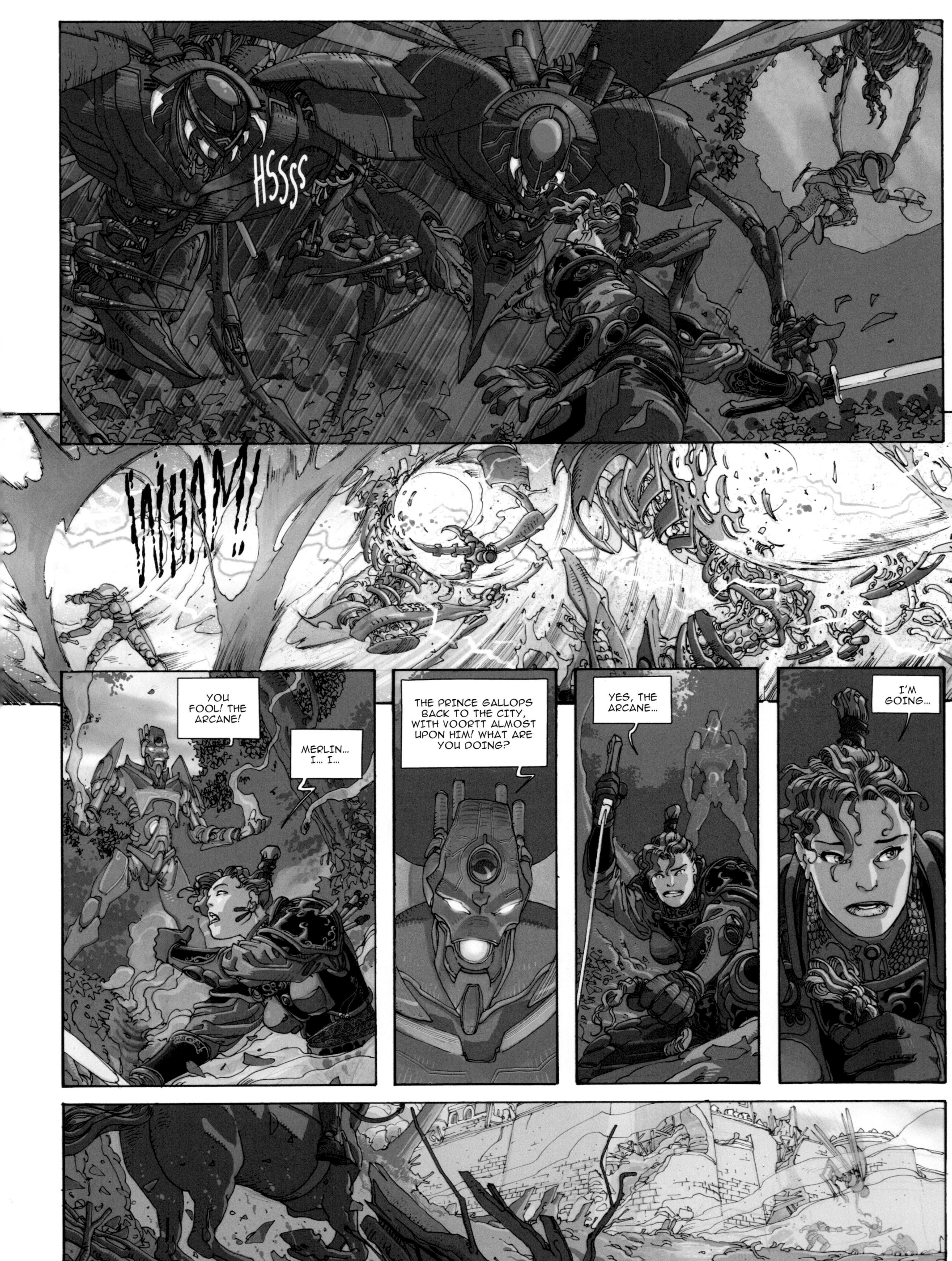
HSSSS
WHAM!!
YOU FOOL! THE ARCANE!
MERLIN... I... I...
THE PRINCE GALLOPS BACK TO THE CITY, WITH VOORTT ALMOST UPON HIM! WHAT ARE YOU DOING?
YES, THE ARCANE...
I'M GOING...

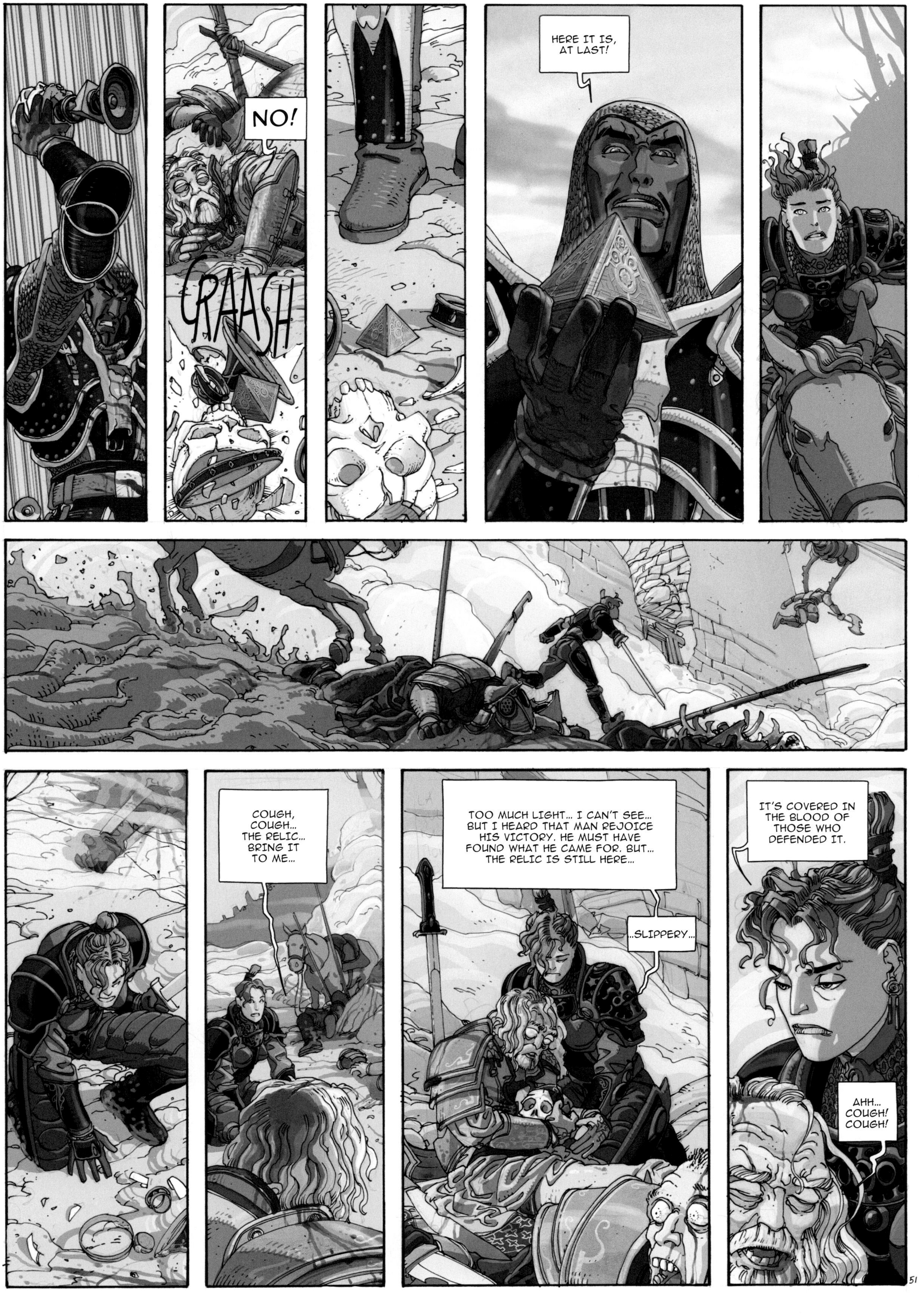
NO!
CRAASH
HERE IT IS, AT LAST!
COUGH, COUGH... THE RELIC... BRING IT TO ME...
TOO MUCH LIGHT... I CAN'T SEE... BUT I HEARD THAT MAN REJOICE HIS VICTORY. HE MUST HAVE FOUND WHAT HE CAME FOR. BUT... THE RELIC IS STILL HERE...
...SLIPPERY...
IT'S COVERED IN THE BLOOD OF THOSE WHO DEFENDED IT.
AHH... COUGH! COUGH!

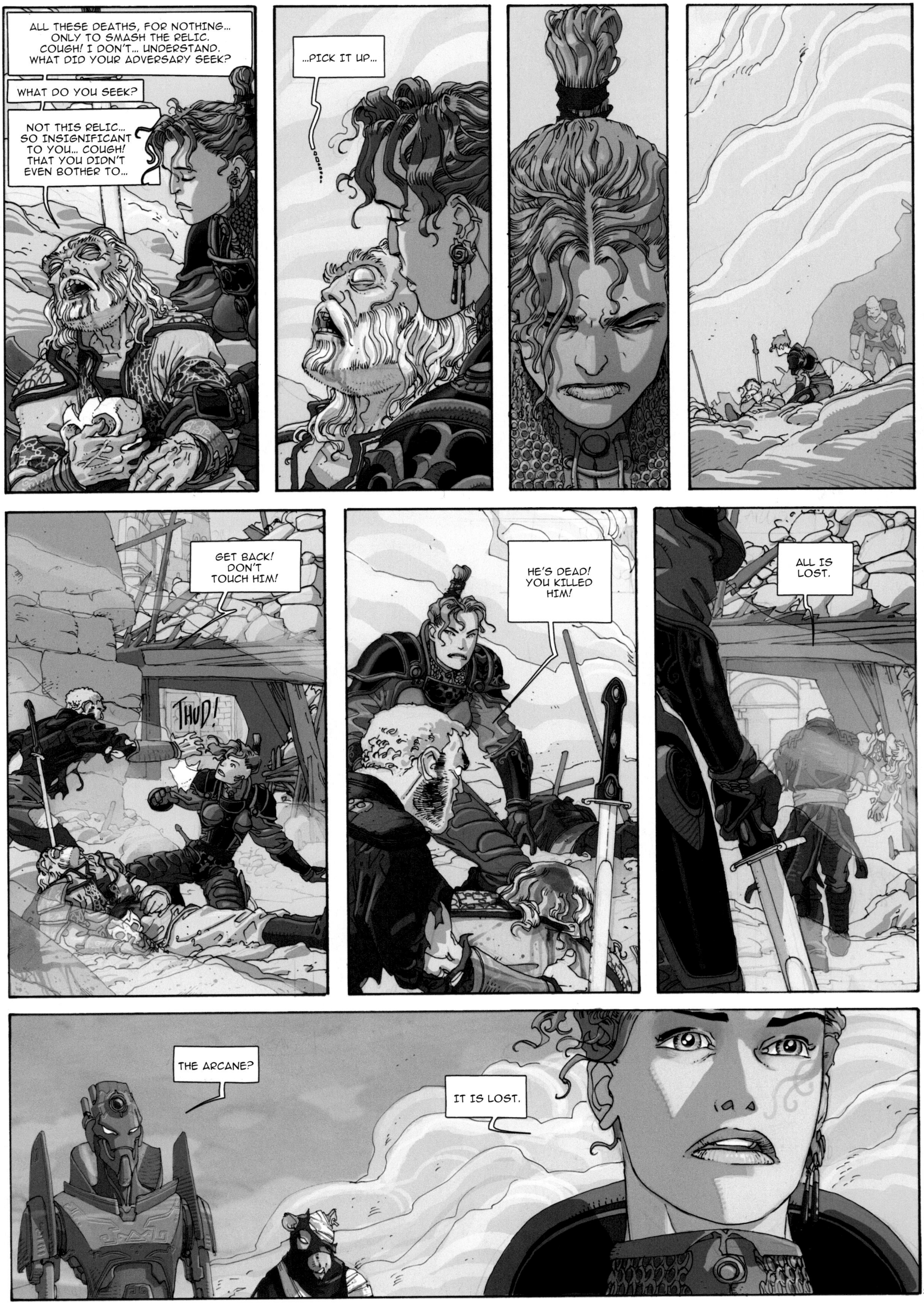

ALL THESE DEATHS, FOR NOTHING... ONLY TO SMASH THE RELIC. COUGH! I DON'T... UNDERSTAND. WHAT DID YOUR ADVERSARY SEEK?
WHAT DO YOU SEEK?
NOT THIS RELIC... SO INSIGNIFICANT TO YOU... COUGH! THAT YOU DIDN'T EVEN BOTHER TO...
...PICK IT UP...
GET BACK! DON'T TOUCH HIM!
THUD!
HE'S DEAD! YOU KILLED HIM!
ALL IS LOST.
THE ARCANE?
IT IS LOST.

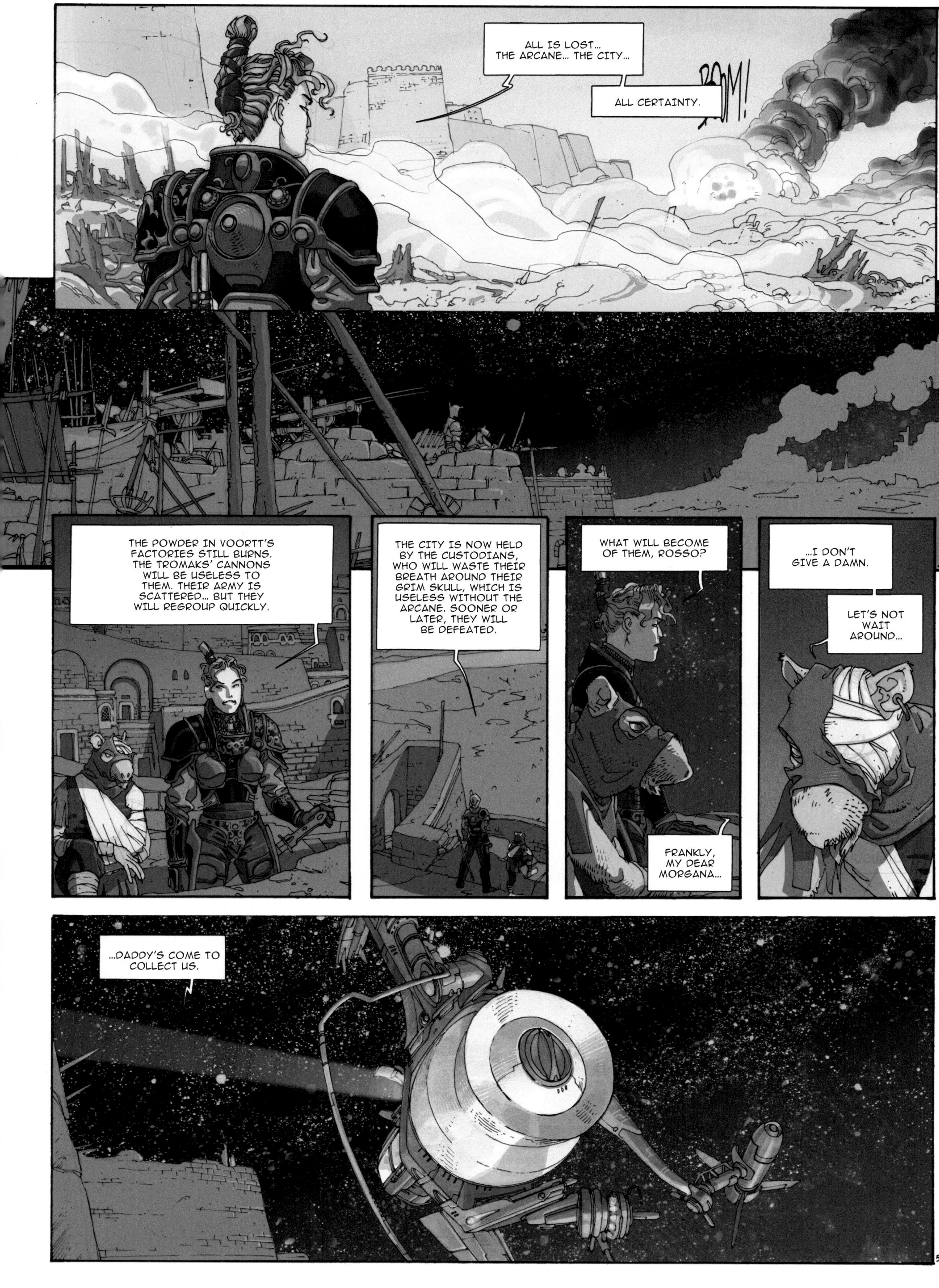
ALL IS LOST... THE ARCANE... THE CITY...
ALL CERTAINTY.
BOOM!
THE POWDER IN VOORTT'S FACTORIES STILL BURNS. THE TROMAKS' CANNONS WILL BE USELESS TO THEM. THEIR ARMY IS SCATTERED... BUT THEY WILL REGROUP QUICKLY.
THE CITY IS NOW HELD BY THE CUSTODIANS, WHO WILL WASTE THEIR BREATH AROUND THEIR GRIM SKULL, WHICH IS USELESS WITHOUT THE ARCANE. SOONER OR LATER, THEY WILL BE DEFEATED.
WHAT WILL BECOME OF THEM, ROSSO?
FRANKLY, MY DEAR MORGANA...
...I DON'T GIVE A DAMN.
LET'S NOT WAIT AROUND...
...DADDY'S COME TO COLLECT US.

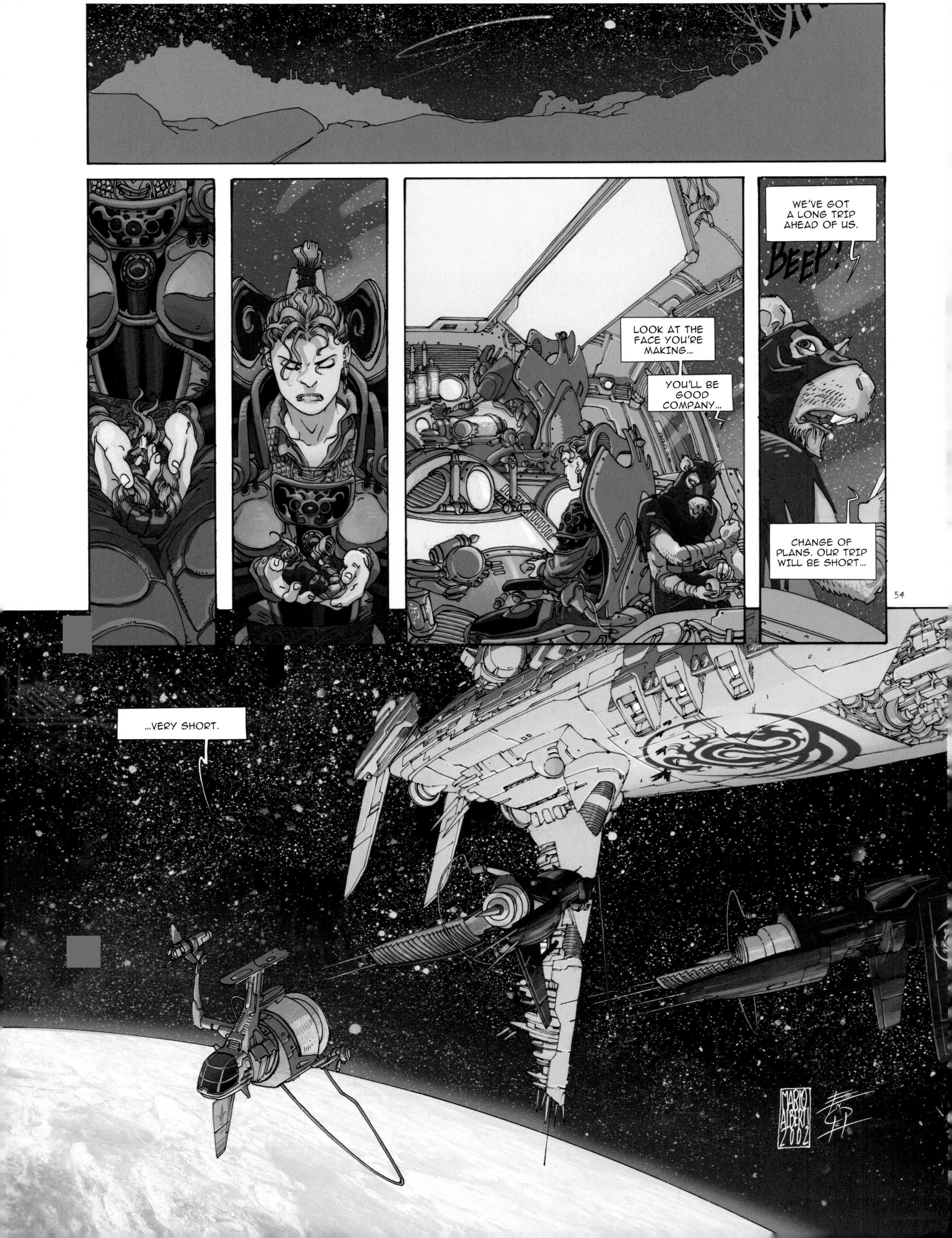
LOOK AT THE FACE YOU'RE MAKING...
YOU'LL BE GOOD COMPANY...
WE'VE GOT A LONG TRIP AHEAD OF US.
BEEP!
CHANGE OF PLANS. OUR TRIP WILL BE SHORT...
...VERY SHORT.
MARIO ALBERTI 2002

ENJOY THOSE OTHER BOOKS FROM
Humanoids Publishing™

 THE NIKOPOL TRILOGY
By Enki Bilal

Hardcover album, Full color,
176 pages. $39.95

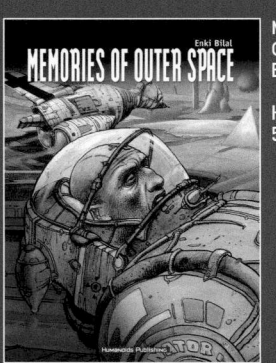 MEMORIES
OF OUTER SPACE
By Enki Bilal

Hardcover album, Full color,
56 pages. $15.95

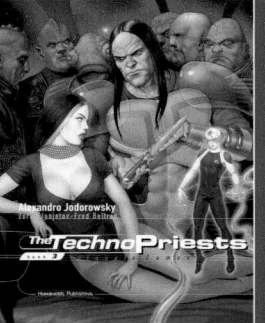 THE TECHNOPRIESTS
VOL.1
VOL.2
VOL.3
By Alexandro Jodorowsky,
Zoran Janjetov & Fred Beltran

Hardcover album, Full color,
56 pages. $14.95

THE FOURTH POWER
By Juan Gimenez

Hardcover album, Full color,
64 pages. $14.95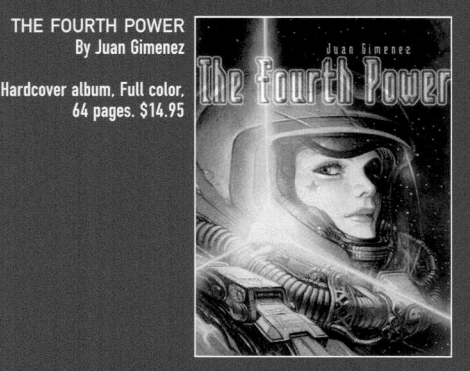

EXTERMINATOR 17
By Enki Bilal
& Jean-Pierre Dionnet

Hardcover album, Full color,
64 pages. $15.95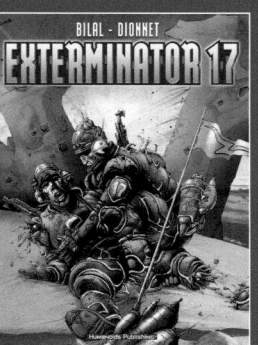

THE DORMANT BEAST
By Enki Bilal

Hardcover album, Full color,
72 pages. $15.95

 FROM CLOUD 99,
MEMORIES PART 1
By Yslaire

Hardcover album, Full color,
64 pages. $14.95

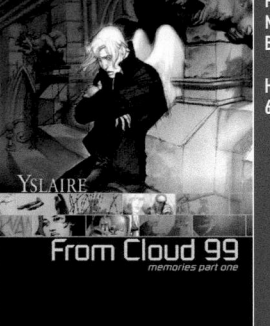 FROM CLOUD 99,
MEMORIES PART 2
By Yslaire

Hardcover album, Full color,
64 pages. $14.95

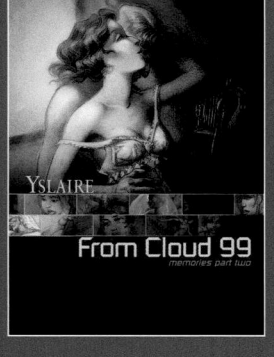 ANTE GENESEM
#1, THE PROPHET
By Xavier Dorison
& Mathieu Lauffray

Hardcover album, Full color,
46 pages. $15.95

METAL HURLANT PRESENTS
PIN-UP GIRLS FROM
AROUND THE WORLD
Art by Fred Beltran

Hardcover album, Full color,
56 pages. $15.95

SON OF THE GUN
VOL.1
By Georges Bess &
Alexandro Jodorowsky

Hardcover album, Full color,
72 pages. $14.95

VOL.2
VOL.3
VOL.4

Hardcover album, Full color,
72 pages. $15.95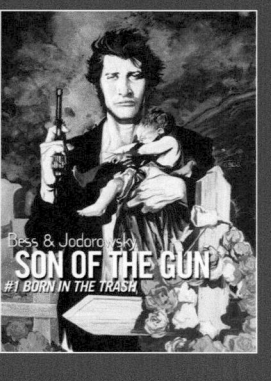

SANCTUM
#1, USS NEBRASKA
By Xavier Dorison
& Christophe Bec

Hardcover album, Full color,
56 pages. $15.95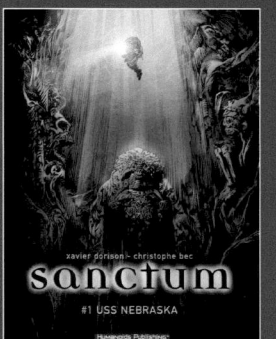

AND MANY MORE...

Available at comic book retailers, your neighborhood book store and quality websites.
Humanoids Publishing • PO Box 931658, Hollywood, CA 90093 • cs@humanoids-publishing.com • www.humanoids-publishing.com